"Education is a natural process carried out by
the human individual, and is acquired not by listening
to words, but by experiences in the environment."

- Maria Montessori

Kids IN THE Kitchen

Simple Recipes
That Build Independence and Confidence
the Montessori Way

Cotner | D'Alton

Table of Contents

Sara's Story

Sara, co-author, with her son, Henry.

My initial journey into the world of Montessori was short-lived. My mother enrolled me in a private Montessori school when I started kindergarten, but she could only afford to send me there until the end of second grade. When it was time to enroll in public school for third grade, we met with an administrator at my new school who talked with us about everything I had learned in my Montessori classroom. Since Montessori schools group children into classrooms with three different grade levels and allow children to work at their own pace, I was a second grader working on third grade material. The administrator at my new school quickly realized that I had already covered most of the third grade objectives and recommended that I skip to fourth grade instead.

I didn't think much about Montessori again until college. My favorite professors sent their children to a local Montessori school, and I decided to observe and write my senior research about my experiences there. After graduation, however, I ventured away from Montessori again, this time to become a third-grade teacher at a high-need school for economically-disadvantaged children in rural Louisiana through a program called Teach For America. At that point, I knew that I wanted to devote my life to making the world a better place through education, and I wanted to work where I was most needed.

Honestly, that little school in the sugar cane fields could not have been farther away from the Montessori approach. The principal kept a paddle on the wall of her office, and she used it. During the middle of a class meeting with my students one day, I heard rhythmic thumping in the hallway and thought that someone was bouncing a basketball down the corridor. When I poked my head out the door, I saw a boy bent over and the principal behind him with her paddle.

In order to avoid sending my students to the principal's office for corporal punishment, I instead relied on positive reinforcement to motivate my students to behave in productive ways, both academically and socially. I passed out raffle tickets to children who embodied our class values and had random drawings throughout the day from the "Super-Duper Jar." The children were also grouped into cooperative learning teams that competed for points and prizes. The list of ways I tried to shape my students' behavior through positive conditioning seems to go on and on! The truth is, it worked. The students in Ms. Cotner's "A+ Class" were motivated, positive, helpful, and hard working.

But then I noticed something strange. When my students graduated from our third-grade classroom and headed into fourth grade, much of their motivation, positivity, persistence, and desire to work hard seemed to evaporate.

After three years of teaching on the bayou, I decided that I wanted to work at a school that used consistent positive motivation across all teachers and all classrooms for several years. I figured that the consistency would help children truly internalize positive behavior and motivation and reach their full potential. I decided to teach sixth-grade reading and writing at a high-performing charter school for economically-disadvantaged children.

I continued to realize, however, that conditioning children with rewards and punishments—even with years of consistency—was still only a temporary solution; it wasn't the way to ensure long-lasting growth and development. Once the person yielding the stickers (the "carrot") or the detention (the "stick") wasn't around, the original behavior returned.

I also started thinking about the idea of the "factory model" of education. With our rows of straight desks and a one-size-fits-all approach, we were perpetuating an outdated model of education that better prepared children for factory work (i.e., following directions, being obedient, doing the same thing at the same time, etc.) versus the ever–changing global economy. On top of that, I attended a lecture by a professor who said, "Our job is not to prepare our children for the 21st century; our job is to prepare our children to transform the 21st century."

I started observing at private schools to look for a better model of education. In 2006, I walked into a fourth-, fifth-, and sixth-grade classroom at a Montessori school in Houston. I saw children happily engaged in different work throughout the classroom. One student was learning decimals by working with hands-on materials on the floor. Another student was talking with the teacher about her goals for the week. There was a snack on the counter that children could help themselves to whenever they were hungry, and there were multiple pets and plants for the children to care for.

Within two minutes, I suspected that Montessori might be the solution I had been searching for to help children develop true motivation and independence from the inside out and to prepare children to be agents of change and the leaders of tomorrow. I knew that my life direction was about to shift course.

I decided to move to Denver to enroll in a Montessori certification program and teach first, second, and third grade at a public Montessori school. I then moved back to Houston and began teaching in a public Montessori program there.

When I got pregnant in 2010, I knew that I wanted to provide our child with a Montessori experience from birth. I started researching how to do Montessori in the home. That's when I found Kylie's blog, HowWeMontessori.com. Even though Kylie lives on the other side of the world (and celebrates Christmas in the summer!), I could immediately see how much we had in common. We both share an immense respect for the Montessori method and try our best to provide an authentic experience for our children at home.

During that time, I became friends with another mom—this time she was right around the corner. Angie and I were both pregnant at the same time and carpooled to prenatal yoga every Monday night. We became fast friends. She was very patient with me as I constantly detailed all the ways I wanted to raise Henry in a Montessori way. Her patience continued after our babies were born and we met every morning at 8:10am for a walk around the neighborhood. I was thrilled when she enrolled her older daughter in the public Montessori school where I had been teaching.

The Montessori approach to guiding the child feels so natural and logical to me, and I started to see positive effects on Henry right away. For example, I followed the recommendations not to bring swings, infant seats, and other common baby contraptions into the home because they can hinder the natural development of movement. Instead, we followed the Montessori approach and set up a movement mat, a

Henry reaching for and grasping some of his Montessori toys.

mobile, and a mirror. Henry spent many hours naturally strengthening his body on that movement mat. In fact, he could roll from his front to his back and his back to his front before he turned three months old.

As he grows, we will continue to provide a Montessori environment, so that he can reach his full potential with regard to focus and concentration, independence and self-confidence, curiosity and lifelong learning, perseverance, global awareness, and empathy and kindness.

I am in the process of creating a network of public Montessori charter schools in diverse communities across the United States called Montessori For All. I want all children to have access to an excellent education, regardless of their parents' income levels. My goal is to have the first school open by the time Henry is three, so he can join the inaugural class.

Kylie's Story

My first son Caspar was only a couple of weeks old when I realized I had no idea how to be a parent. Sure I knew how to feed and wash him, but I didn't know how to play with him or how we should spend our days. I had given up a rewarding career to stay at home with him; I wanted to give him the best, but I didn't know how. When he was only a couple of months old, I had enrolled him in every baby class available. We were attending baby swim, gym, music, and playgroup every day of the week. We were busy and unhappy; I knew there was a better way. I started researching parenting philosophies and was immediately drawn to Montessori. Fostering independence, following the child, order and consistency—it made sense to me.

Kylie, co-author and photographer, with her sons, Caspar and Otis.

However, I found implementing Montessori in the home really difficult. I felt isolated. I had researched Montessori using only the resources at our local library. I knew I wanted to create a Montessori home environment, but I didn't know how.

After Caspar turned one, we moved to Canberra, a move which changed our lives. I met other Montessori families, enrolled in a parent–toddler class, and met wonderful Montessori teachers. The teachers at our local school had the greatest impact on me. In them I found patience, passion, and true love of the child.

Caspar is now four and he still attends a Montessori school. We have a second child, Otis, who has just turned one. Otis has been raised from birth in a Montessori way.

Now I devote much of my time to writing and communicating with Montessori parents around the world. From the basics to the fine detail, sharing information is empowering.

Angie's Story

Angie, book designer, with her daughters, Sofia and Ana.

In an effort to build community within our neighborhood, Sara and her husband invited our entire street over for an informal potluck gathering. I don't remember much about that first meeting with Sara, but I remember she was gracious enough to loan me a film she had recently watched that had inspired her. I left there with a DVD copy of *Edison's Day*, a short documentary chronicling the day of a young boy whose parents follow Montessori principles. Edison was twenty months—about the same age as my daughter, Sofia. I was blown away by the amount of respect these parents had for their young child's capabilities. Edison helped dress and undress himself, prepared his breakfast, and even got the morning paper from the front step!

The biggest connection I made while watching the video was that encouragement of your child's independence leads to solid core confidence in the child. It resonated so deeply with me and inspired me to cultivate that independence in Sofia and then later in Ana, our second daughter. It changed the way I parent and it showed me the things that I was already doing right—one of which was cooking with my children from a young age.

When it came time to research preschools, Sara and I connected again. This time we were both pregnant, she with her first and I with my second. She was sharing with me all that she was learning about Montessori for infants and setting up a Montessori environment in the home. She also shared with me about how lucky we are in Houston, to have a Montessori option in the public school system. Sofia, now four, is thriving beyond my expectations in her first year of preschool there. My hope, like Sara's, is that children of all socioeconomic classes can have access to the thoughtful, engaging method of education that is Montessori.

Overview of What to Expect

Our children are usually capable of way more than we give them credit for. I learned this lesson (and continue to learn it) frequently. For example, I was reading one of Kylie's blog posts about how her son Otis feeds himself with a spoon. Since Henry is a month older than Otis, I realized it might be time to teach him how to use a spoon. I slowly modeled how I dip the spoon into the yogurt and bring it to my mouth. I then handed the spoon to him and he immediately scooped up some yogurt and maneuvered the spoon straight to his mouth. To my astonishment, I realized he already knew how to do it; I was the one holding him back!

Kylie's son, Otis, feeding himself with a spoon, at 12 months. Courtesy of Kylie's blog, How We Montessori.

Kylie had a similar experience when she read on my blog, FeedingTheSoil.com, that Henry had started helping in the kitchen shortly after his first birthday. She decided to see if Otis was ready, too. She sliced a banana into discs, made an additional cut in the peel, and showed Otis how to peel each piece. He took to it right away.

When we step back to give children a chance to do things for themselves, we allow them to contribute to their own self-formation. We help them cultivate the deepest and most authentic sense of self-worth. They feel proud of themselves because they witness their own ability to impact the world around them—not because they receive praise from adults. And isn't that what we want for our children? For them to have a solid core of self-confidence that will give them the courage to live their best lives?

Even the youngest child can work in the kitchen with the right guidance. This book provides that guidance. First, we enumerate all the ways in which your child will grow and develop from working in the kitchen in the "Why Cook with Your Child?" chapter. Next, we explain "How to Use This Book," with specific strategies to keep in mind in order to be the best "guide on the side" possible. Then we delve into the specific details of setting up your home kitchen environment in a way that will maximize your child's independence, in the chapter called "Setting Up the Kitchen." After that, we get started with the specific skills that you can teach your child in order to prepare them to cook with more confidence and independence. Then your child will be ready to try out the simple, step-by-step recipes. They will experience an enormous sense of accomplishment through the process of looking at the pictures, following each step, eating their creations, and sharing them with others.

Why Cook with Your Child?

According to Maria Montessori's theory of development, children spend the first six years of their lives in the "Absorbent Mind" period. During this time, they internalize the environment and the experiences around them to form their personalities. As the primary adults in our children's lives, we have the opportunity to provide them with the kind of environment and experiences that will help them develop into their best possible selves.

The time we have with our children is a zero-sum game. Every minute they spend doing something is a minute they are not doing something else. For example, if they spend an hour watching TV they are not building their fine- or gross-motor skills, developing language by talking with another person, or participating in the daily rhythm of life to feel like an authentic contributor to the family.

As important as it is to engage our children in meaningful experiences, we might struggle to make time for it. We might be working full-time, doing piles of laundry, trying to find time to connect with our partners and friends—the list goes on. Fortunately, involving our children in the day-to-day activities of the home (e.g., cooking, cleaning, doing laundry, etc.) means that we get to check items off our to-do lists and engage with our children in ways that positively impact their development. Yes, it takes more patience and time to involve kids in the practical chores of the home, but we accomplish two goals at once: we keep the house in order and we help our children feel like valuable, useful, contributing members of the household. Bringing your child into the kitchen to cook with you (from a very early age!) will help your child develop:

A Willingness to Try Diverse Foods Children seem to be much more open to trying (and liking) foods that they help prepare.

Numeracy and Literacy Following recipes and cooking helps children learn math and reading in authentic contexts.

Critical Thinking and Problem-Solving While cooking, children are constantly faced with new situations and challenges that require them to think more deeply and creatively.

Fine-Motor Skills Actions like grating, slicing, and pouring help children gain mastery over their hands.

Independence Cooking provides children with an authentic opportunity to cultivate their ability to do things for themselves.

Self Confidence and Sense of Self There's something incredibly powerful about being able to make something for yourself. Creating something with your own two hands can help cultivate the deepest kind of confidence and the strongest sense of self.

Focus and Concentration Cooking-related activities— like following recipes accurately or pouring from one container to another—help children strengthen their ability to focus and concentrate on the task at hand.

Intrinsic Motivation When children engage in activities that result in a desired outcome—like following a recipe and making a pizza to eat—they cultivate intrinsic motivation. They see that hard work and perseverance are worth it. They begin to do things for their own sake rather than to receive external praise. This pattern sets them up for a lifetime of being motivated from within.

Regional and Seasonal Knowledge Working in the kitchen helps children acclimate to their particular place and time as they learn about the foods around them.

Participation in Cultural and Social Events Cooking is a central part of most cultures and participating in the process helps place children at the center of the important events in our family and culture.

Fun and Enjoyment Very simply, children find immense pleasure in doing adult work. They want to be next to us as we stir, knead bread, or grate cheese.

Involving your child in food preparation can help improve their fine motor skills.

How to Use This Book

We intentionally designed this book as a "one–stop shop" for cooking with your children. It includes everything you need to know about preparing a kitchen environment that supports your child's development. Once you have set up the kitchen in a way that aligns with your child's needs, then you can teach them the first skill. The skills and the recipes have been intentionally sequenced to progress in the most logical way according to child development. The skills are the foundation upon which the recipes are built. Once your child is comfortable executing all the different skills, then it is time to introduce the first recipe.

The recipes are intentionally simple, which will allow your child to follow them with as much independence as possible. We illustrate each step of the process with a photograph, so your child can follow along, even without being able to read. When your child is ready to start reading, we provide corresponding text with simple words and phrases to support literacy development.

There are safety concerns when cooking with children, as well as instances where the child will require assistance from an adult. We have created a symbol to alert the child that adult supervision is necessary.

Once you've equipped your kitchen in a way that supports your child and taught them the basic skills required for the recipes, it's time to step back and let your child work. As Maria Montessori said, "Never help a child with a task at which [s]he feels [s]he can succeed." It might be tempting to jump in when your child is attempting to pour the pancake batter on the griddle and is spilling a little on the counter. Resist! Your child is doing the very important work of forming themselves. They are developing confidence, intrinsic motivation, and a strong sense of self. After they finish pouring all the pancakes, then you can teach them how to clean up spills. That

Be sure your child knows this symbol means adult supervision is necessary.

process will be an important part of their self-formation, too.

If you notice that your child has trouble with a particular skill, resist the urge to "fix" the problem in the moment. Instead, make a mental note of what your child needs additional practice with and then find opportunities at a later time to give them a little extra practice with the skill in a more isolated context. The more you step back and resist the urge to interfere, the more your child will learn. Of course you want to provide the right amount of support when they need it in order to avoid too much challenge or frustration, but you want to give them the space they need to figure out things on their own. Let them figure out how to solve issues that come up. They often need more thinking time than we do, but their solutions can be just as valid as (or even better than) our own.

When your child does need support, figure out how to provide the least amount possible. Rather than provide the answer, try asking a question. Instead of taking over and doing it yourself, offer a suggestion or modeling it withseparate materials. Teaching children to do things for themselves can be an incredibly difficult experience that requires an overwhelming amount of patience and self-awareness. I try to remind myself that, as Gretchen Rubin says, "the days are long, but the years are short." We are given a relatively short window of time to help develop the core of our child's personality.

How to Set Up the Kitchen

The "Prepared Environment" is an important aspect of the Montessori philosophy. As adults, we have the opportunity to set up the physical space in a way that facilitates the child's innate drive to learn. For example, when our children are learning to crawl, we can put interesting toys just beyond their reach that roll slightly when touched. As we are cultivating their confidence and competence in the kitchen, we can prepare the environment in a way that maximizes their independence. This section addresses the major areas of preparation: apron, materials, storage, and the preparation area.

Apron The first step in setting up the kitchen is finding a suitable apron for your child. An apron doesn't only protect clothing; it helps to define the activity. While wearing the apron, the child is reminded that they are cooking. Taking off and putting away the apron concludes the activity.

Cloth (left) or oil cloth (right) aprons should be child-sized. Velcro straps allow children to fasten the apron themselves and help facilitate independence.

Putting on and taking off the apron by themselves is an important step. It sets the scene and tells the child that they are capable and independent.

The apron is to be used for cooking only. If you use an apron for art activities or gardening, ensure it is different in appearance and stored separately. We have both cloth and oilcloth aprons. Oilcloth is ideal for a child who loves to splash or spends a lot of time with water.

For a cloth apron, we suggest a neckband that is elastic or large enough to easily go over the child's head and a waist strap that fastens with Velcro. Oilcloth aprons can be made with an opening to pull over the head and a simple strap that fastens with Velcro at the front.

When making or purchasing an apron, consider the size of your child. Some aprons can be folded or hemmed so they do not drag on the floor. We have found children's aprons generally come in two sizes: 18 months–3 years and 3 years and over.

Pride of ownership is important. Ensure you and your child check the apron for cleanliness and launder when necessary.

Using real utensils is important. Child-sized utensils are easier to hold and control.

Utensils As with anything we provide our children, utensils used in the kitchen must be real. Real tools send a message to the child that they are about to do real and important work.

In many instances, child-sized utensils are recommended. They are smaller and lighter than adult versions, making them easier to hold and control. A comparison of mixing spoons and whisks illustrates the difference.

We also look for the easiest tools for the child to use. For example, a young child will find ice tongs easier than adult tongs with a latch, or a small mixing bowl with a handle and non-slip base easier than a large mixing bowl.

Small serving dishes and a tray for sharing are nice touches. As your child progresses, there is a whole range of materials you can invest in. When I am in kitchen supply shops, I keep my eyes open for sales, new products, and ideas. We didn't set up our kitchen quickly, but rather over time accumulated bits and pieces. Look for the best quality you can afford.

When you are ready to introduce cooking with heat, start with a small skillet with a cool–touch handle on an electric stove top or a small electric skillet.

Children should also be given the opportunity to clean up any mess or spills. An adult sponge cut in half and moistened, cleaning cloths, and a child-sized dustpan and broom will assist with most cleaning tasks. We have a small spray bottle filled with water for additional cleaning, a broom, mop, compost bin, and small laundry basket. It's good practice to demonstrate cleaning activities such as wiping down counters, sweeping, and washing dishes from early on.

If your child enjoys wiping dishes, consider a small tea towel or cutting and hemming an adult-sized towel. We also recommend using environmentally friendly cloth napkins and find lunch or cocktail sized napkins ideal.

An orderly drawer ensures utensils have a specific spot; low shelves help provide easy access to materials.

Storage To assist with your child's independence, place their materials in an area that is as accessible as possible. Ensure all materials have a specific spot, a place where the child can routinely locate the items and remember to put them back after use.

A low hook can be used to hang an apron. If the apron cannot hang on a hook, consider neatly folding the apron and storing it on a low shelf or drawer.

Cooking materials can be stored on a low shelf or drawer. For those with small kitchens it can be difficult finding the right space. Some families find a small shelf placed at the end of the kitchen works or even in a small container in the pantry. As much as possible, keep the storage area clean and uncluttered. Cutlery trays, baskets, or caddies can help to keep utensils orderly.

To further assist your child's independence, eating utensils, a plate, a bowl, drinking glass, napkins, and placemats could be kept within easy reach. Once your child is ready for the responsibility, consider placing snacks within his or her reach. This provides the opportunity to show freedom within limits. We recommend only allowing access to healthy foods in small quantities, only to be accessed during defined snack times. This could extend to the bottom shelf of the refrigerator door to store cut up fruit, vegetable sticks, cheese, or yogurt. It is important to note this works very well for some children while for others it will always be too much temptation.

Low hanging hooks are good for storing brooms, dustpans, and mops. Throughout our home, we find temporary hooks useful. They can be used without damaging the wall surface and can be raised as the child grows.

Preparation Area When cooking, the comfort and safety of the child are paramount. Some children will like to work seated or standing at a child-sized table. However we have found that our children like to work near us at the kitchen table or counter. Older children can access the counter with a stable step stool. For younger children, we highly recommend a device such as a Learning Tower or Fun Pod. Many of the skills require coordination and strength. It is important for the child to be at a comfortable working height and feel stable.

Setting up the prepared environment in a way that supports your child's independence takes time and creativity. Be patient with the process as you convert your adult-sized kitchen into a space that welcomes and honors the child.

Skills

When your child is ready to learn a new skill, start by giving a demonstration.

☐ Use your actions to guide your child. Demonstrate the skill slowly. Be precise and consider carefully where you place your hands. Demonstrate the skill while next to your child. This makes it easier for them to copy your movements. Allow your child to observe closely and without distraction. At first demonstrate in silence or use words for emphasis only.

☐ Consider your child's dominant hand. If you are uncertain as to which hand your child will use, let them take the lead. For example, put the knife on the chopping board and ask your child to pick it up. The hand they pick it up with is likely to be the hand they will use to cut.

☐ Be patient—some skills are easier than others. If your child isn't interested, finds a skill too difficult, or is discouraged, be prepared to put it away and leave it for a week or longer until you feel your child is ready.

Remember, there are many ways to perform each skill. Take time to think about what would work in your family, taking into consideration the foods you eat and the equipment you have.

Washing Most fruits and vegetables will need to be washed before they are used. Some will need a rinse and others will need a scrub with a vegetable brush. A brush that fits into the palm of your child's hand is perfect for scrubbing.

☐ Take the brush in the dominant hand.

☐ Hold the vegetable in the other hand.

☐ Use a circular motion to remove dirt from the vegetable.

☐ A sieve or colander can be used for rinsing.

Washing is an ideal activity for a child who enjoys water play. You can fill the sink or a tub and let them scrub away. Have a towel nearby for cleaning up.

Pouring It is easiest for a child to pour with a pitcher that can be comfortably held in one hand. If your child finds this skill difficult, consider using a smaller pitcher.

☐ Hold the handle of the pitcher with the dominant hand.

☐ Support the bottom of the pitcher with the other hand.

☐ Slowly pour the ingredients from the pitcher.

Pouring can be practiced from pitcher to pitcher. Start with pouring items such as beans or rice. As your child progresses, move onto pouring liquids such as water.

Once your child has mastered this skill, consider placing a water pitcher and a drinking glass on a low table, so they can help themselves when they are thirsty. Alternatively, provide a pitcher and glass at mealtime to allow your child to independently pour their own drink.

To begin, provide your child with a small amount of food, such as a few crackers and a small bowl of hummus. Examples we enjoy include rice cakes, bread, or toast spread with cream cheese, peanut butter, jam, or mashed banana. You can purchase specialized spreaders for this purpose. A small butter knife can also work well.

- ☐ Hold the knife with the dominant hand.
- ☐ Scoop up some of the spread onto the knife.
- ☐ Hold the cracker still with the other hand.
- ☐ Move the knife across the cracker, evenly distributing the spread.

Once your child has mastered this skill, they are able to independently prepare their own snack. If you are expecting guests, consider placing the prepared crackers on a plate and offering them on arrival. This can be a great lesson in grace and courtesy and makes for a warm welcome.

Find a knife your child is comfortable with and use it regularly. If a child is cutting infrequently or using a different knife each time, it can become difficult for them to master the skill. It is easier for the child to cut food that sits flat on the chopping board. For example, cut carrots and potatoes in half first so they don't roll or move for the child.

A child can be shown to safely use a small paring knife. Pressing down on the top of the knife ensures fingers are out of the way. If the knife is serrated, show the child to hold the food while slicing. Close supervision is needed.

- ☐ Hold the knife with the dominant hand.
- ☐ Hold the food with the other hand.
- ☐ Use a down-cut action to slice the food.

Soft fruits are good for learning to cut. Bananas, for example, are easy to cut with a small bread knife or crinkle cutter, shown below, right.

Apple slicers are a popular tool for slicing apples and other fruits like pears. You may need to press the slicer into the fruit an inch or so to get the slicer started for your child.

- ☐ Hold the slicer with both hands over the fruit.
- ☐ Press down firmly and evenly with both hands.
- ☐ Take the apple pieces from the slicer.

Once your child is slicing foods, you may want to introduce the use of tongs to transfer the food to a plate or serving tray. Small tongs are essential for the child's small hands. Ice tongs are good; they are very easy to use to grip and pick up foods. For practice, we suggest slicing a banana, transferring the pieces onto a plate, and then putting a toothpick into each piece to share at snack time. Cheese is also a good choice for slicing and sharing.

- ☐ Hold the tongs in the dominant hand.
- ☐ Squeeze fingers and thumb together to pick up an item in the tongs.
- ☐ Transfer the item to a plate and release with the hand.

Mixing is easiest for the child when using a child-sized bowl and spoon. Don't be concerned about how the child holds the mixing spoon; they will naturally find the most comfortable way.

- ☐ Hold the mixing spoon in the dominant hand.
- ☐ Hold the bowl with the other hand.
- ☐ Mix with the spoon in a circular motion.

Mashing

When learning to mash, it is easiest to work with small quantities of food such as one piece of fruit or a cup equivalent.

Mashed fruit mixed with a cup of yogurt is both an easy snack for a child to prepare independently and a great way to reinforce mashing and mixing skills.

- ☐ Hold the masher with the dominant hand.
- ☐ Hold the bowl with the other hand.
- ☐ Press down into the fruit with the masher and repeat.

Whisking

A child-sized whisk is easier for the child to hold and coordinate.

- ☐ Hold the whisk in the dominant hand.
- ☐ Hold the bowl in the other hand.
- ☐ Using a small circular motion, whisk the ingredients.

Peeling

Observe how you hold the peeler before demonstrating to your child. Different peelers require a different hand grip. A carrot is a good choice for demonstrating peeling. If peeling a carrot, it is easiest to leave the leaves on for the child to hold.

- ☐ Hold the peeler in the dominant hand.
- ☐ Hold the food to be peeled in the other hand.
- ☐ Take the peeler and start from the top. Use a downwards stroke and then repeat.

While your child is learning to sift, be prepared for some mess. We suggest using a large bowl to capture the sifted material. Flour is an obvious choice for practicing sifting. If you have more than a cup to sift, it may be easier for the child to continue sifting and an adult to refill the sifter.

A sieve can work well for younger children.

☐ Hold the sieve in the dominant hand.

☐ Pour food into the sieve.

☐ Move the sieve up and down or tap on the side of the bowl.

If using a sifter, we recommend using one that is child-sized. A child-sized sifter is lighter and the proportions make it easier for the child to hold and turn the handle.

☐ Hold the sifter in the non-dominant hand.

☐ Pour food into the sifter.

☐ Use a circular motion to turn the handle of the sifter with the dominant hand.

Until your child is proficient in cutting, it is best to provide the fruit already cut in half. Citrus fruits are most commonly juiced this way. Depending on the juicer used you may want to remove the seeds from the fruit first.

☐ Hold the fruit with the dominant hand; place onto the juicer.

☐ Use the other hand to hold the handle of the juicer.

☐ Press the fruit down onto the juicer and rotate with the wrist to remove juice from the fruit.

Juicing (cont.)

Other juicing devices, like a juicing squeezer, can be fun to try.

☐ Place fruit into the juicing squeezer.

☐ Use both hands to press the juicing squeezer together.

☐ Hold the juicing squeezer over bowl so that juice is squeezed out of the fruit into the bowl.

This juicing reamer is quick and easy when juicing smaller fruits such as lemons or limes.

☐ Hold the reamer in the dominant hand.

☐ Hold the fruit in the other hand.

☐ Hold both hands over a bowl and use a pressing and twisting motion to insert the reamer into the fruit to remove the juice.

Grating

To set up the child for success with grating, ensure the food is cut so that it easily fits in the child's hand. Carrots and cheese are good options for grating. Both can contribute to a salad or sandwich filling.

☐ Hold the grater in the non-dominant hand.

☐ Hold the food in the dominant hand.

☐ Use an up and down motion to grate the food.

Specialized cheese graters can be fun and challenging. This grater requires strength and coordination.

☐ Place the cheese in the grater.

☐ Grip the grater handle.

☐ Rotate the grater with the other hand.

Using a garlic press requires strength and can be difficult for a child. To make it slightly easier, cut the garlic into pieces before putting it in the garlic press.

- ☐ Place the garlic into the garlic press.
- ☐ Hold the garlic press with two hands.
- ☐ Squeeze the handles together and crush the garlic.

A mortar and pestle can be fun for a child, albeit a little noisy. If you are using fresh herbs, a quick crush in the mortar and pestle can help release the flavors.

- ☐ Place the food/herbs into the mortar and hold the pestle in the dominant hand.
- ☐ Hold the mortar with the other hand.
- ☐ Depending on the desired texture of the food, tap and grind the food with the pestle.

We suggest using a measuring cup and foods such as rice or beans to demonstrate dry measuring. This is a fun activity to try with sand in the sand box or even in a sensory tub. Once your child has mastered this, move on to measuring smaller amounts like a tablespoon or a teaspoon if using finer foods like flour.

- ☐ Hold the measuring cup in the non-dominant hand.
- ☐ Scoop up some of the dry ingredient.
- ☐ Hold a knife in the dominant hand and with the back of the knife level off the measuring cup.

Measuring Wet Ingredients

When measuring more than a cup, a measuring pitcher is a good option. It can be fun for children to practice measuring liquids using colored water. Measuring liquids is also an activity that can be performed at a water table.

☐ Pour the liquid slowly into the measuring pitcher to the desired fill line.

☐ Check the measurement at eye level and add or pour liquid out to be accurate.

Kneading

Kneading is a difficult skill to master and takes practice and time. Most importantly your child will need to build up their hand strength. We suggest practicing kneading with a small ball of soft, homemade play dough. You should also knead alongside your child as they will need to constantly refer to your movements.

☐ Place both hands on the top of the ball of dough.

☐ Push the heel of the hands (base of the palm) down into the ball and out.

☐ Fold the dough over from the top and repeat the process.

Our favorite homemade play dough recipe:

½ c Flour
½ c Water
¼ c Salt
½ T Cream of tartar
½ t Cooking oil

1. Combine and mix ingredients over low heat.
2. Cool and knead.

This makes one small ball.

Cracking an egg can be a lot of fun, but you don't want to waste too many eggs practicing. Scrambled eggs or omelettes are good options for using up eggs.

☐ Tap the egg against the edge of the bowl (or counter) to create a crack.

☐ Place both thumbs in the crack.

☐ Pull the egg apart into the bowl.

When learning to flip, it is best to start with a solid food such as a slice of bread or a pancake made of soft play dough.

Flipping

☐ Take the spatula in the dominant hand.

☐ Slide the spatula under the food.

☐ Lift and tip the food so that it flips over.

Setting a Timer

A manual dial timer is helpful for a child if they are still grasping the concept of time. The dial also helps the child make a connection to time on a clock.

☐ Hold the base of the timer with one hand.

☐ Turn the dial to the desired time point with the other hand.

Cooking with Heat

Introduce your child to cooking with heat by starting with a skillet on an electric stove top or using an electric skillet. Using a medium heat allows the skillet to heat enough to cook but reduces the risk of injury. Cooking French toast is a fun way to cook with heat and to practice flipping. Don't forget to turn the skillet or stove top off.

☐ Turn the skillet/stove top to medium heat and add the food to the skillet.

☐ Hold the spatula or mixing spoon in the dominant hand and hold the (cool to the touch) handle of the skillet with the other hand.

☐ Mix/flip the foods as desired and until cooked. Lift and tip the food so that it flips over.

Recipes

Fruit Salad

This sweet and healthy side dish makes a great addition to breakfast, lunch, or dinner or can stand on its own as a snack or light dessert.

Gather Ingredients

1 Slice watermelon
1 Orange
1 c Mixed berries, such as strawberries and blueberries
1 Mango
Fresh mint leaves
1 T Honey

1 Wash berries.

2 Cut strawberries into bite-sized pieces.

3 Place strawberries and blueberries into a bowl.

4 Cut mango and slice one half into bite-sized pieces.

5 Add mango to the bowl.

6 Cut watermelon into bite-sized pieces.

7 Add watermelon to the bowl.

Add seasonal fruits, such as a banana or apple for variety.

Try This!

8 Juice half an orange.

9 Add orange juice to bowl.

10 Add honey to bowl.

11 Tear and add mint leaves to bowl.

12 Mix and serve.

Tips for Adults

You can increase or decrease the difficulty of this recipe depending upon how much preparation you do with the fruit.

Tzatziki Dip

This refreshing dip packs the protein and provides more incentive to snack on vegetables.

Gather Ingredients

1 c Natural or Greek
  style yogurt
1 Medium cucumber
1 Lemon
1 Small clove garlic

| Wash cucumber.

2 Remove tip from cucumber.

3 Grate cucumber.

4 Use a clean cloth to pat the grated cucumber dry.

5 Place cucumber into a bowl.

6 Juice half a lemon.

Serve with whole wheat crackers or vegetable sticks. Dips make vegetables more enticing and fun to eat.

Try This!

7 Add lemon juice to bowl.

8 Crush garlic into bowl.

9 Add yogurt to bowl.

10 Mix and serve.

Tips for Adults

If your child doesn't like the taste of garlic, leave it out and simply make a refreshing cucumber dip.

Pizza

*Always a popular option, this pizza recipe is sure to please,
while providing a balanced and healthy meal.*

Gather Ingredients

1 T Tomato paste
1 Tomato
1 Piece whole wheat
  pita bread
Mozzarella cheese
Fresh basil leaves

1 Wash tomato.

2 Slice tomato.

3 Grate cheese.

4 Place pita bread on baking tray and spread with tomato paste.

5 Place tomato and cheese onto pita bread.

6 Tear and place basil on top of pita bread.

7 Have an adult bake in the oven at 350°F or 180°C for 10 minutes.

Tips for Adults

Once your child is comfortable with this basic recipe, increase the challenge by having them make the dough from scratch.

Carrot & Apple Salad

The perfect blend of fruits and vegetables, this light and airy salad will make mouths smile.

Gather Ingredients

1 Carrot
1 Apple

1 Wash carrot and apple.

2 Cut apple.

3 Grate apple.

4 Place apple in bowl.

5 Peel carrot.

6 Grate carrot.

Add shredded celery for tang or golden raisins for sweetness.

Try This!

7 Add carrot to bowl.

8 Mix and serve.

Tips for Adults

If you don't have an apple slicer, you could slice the apple for the child with a knife.

Cutting the tip off of the carrot first can make shredding easier.

If the child is having difficulty grating the apple, try peeling it first.

Banana & Strawberry Muffins

These moist and delicious muffins provide a healthy alternative to cupcakes and other sugary treats. This recipe yields 24 mini-muffins.

Gather Ingredients

¼ c Milk
1 Banana
1 Egg
4 Strawberries
1 c Whole wheat
self-rising flour
½ c Honey yogurt

1 Wash strawberries.

2 Cut strawberries into small pieces and add to bowl.

3 Peel and mash banana.

4 Crack egg and add to bowl.

5 Add milk to bowl.

6 Add yogurt to bowl.

Add chopped nuts or substitute other berries, such as raspberries or blueberries.

Try This!

7 Add flour to bowl.

8 Mix all ingredients well.

9 Place cupcake liners into muffin tray.

10 Spoon mixture into cupcake liners.

11 Have an adult bake in the oven at 350°F or 180°C for 20 minutes.

Tips for Adults

If you don't have cupcake liners, simply grease the muffin tray.

If you don't have honey yogurt, try using plain yogurt and adding honey.

Basic Bread

This versatile recipe can be used for sandwiches, toast, croutons—the ideas are endless!

Gather Ingredients

1½ c Warm water
1½ T Dried yeast
4 c Whole wheat flour
¼ c Olive oil
¼ c Honey
1½ t Salt

1 Add yeast and honey to warm water.

2 Mix to dissolve and set aside.

3 Measure and add flour to bowl.

4 Add salt to bowl.

5 Mix.

6 Make a well in the center of the bowl.

7 Add oil.

8 Add warm water, honey, and yeast mixture to bowl.

9 Mix well until the dough forms a ball.

10 Flour the counter (or work surface).

11 Place dough on floured surface and knead for approximately five minutes.

12 Add dough to bowl.

13 Cover bowl with a warm towel and leave in a warm place.

14 Set timer for 20 minutes and check dough until it has doubled in size.

15 Remove risen dough from bowl and briefly knead the dough.

Divide the dough into six balls for perfectly-sized dinner rolls, or add cinnamon and raisins for a fruit bread treat.

Try This!

16 Shape the dough into a loaf.

17 Place the dough on a baking tray.

18 Have an adult place in the oven at 350°F or 180°C for 30 minutes or until brown.

19 Allow to cool and serve.

Tips for Adults

Kneading can be very difficult for children. Consider halving the dough and kneading alongside them.

See the Skills section for more tips on kneading.

Mini Berry Pancakes

Your child can serve up breakfast with this simple and delicious recipe for pancakes.

Gather Ingredients

¾ c Milk
1 Egg
1 c Whole wheat
   self-rising flour
½ c Fresh berries,
   such as blueberries

1 Wash berries.

2 Crack egg into a large bowl.

3 Add milk.

4 Whisk egg and milk until combined.

5 Sift a small amount of flour into bowl.

6 Whisk flour. Continue to sift more flour and whisk until combined.

Experiment with other toppings, such as nuts or peanut butter.

Try This!

7 Add berries.

8 Pour small amount of mixture into pan at medium heat.

9 Cook until bubbles form. Then flip.

10 Serve.

Tips for Adults

Help your child find the easiest way to pour a small amount of batter into the pan, such as using a measuring cup.

The smaller the pancakes, the easier they will be to flip independently.

Vegetable Ribbons

Beautiful and nutritious, this vegetable side dish makes a great addition to dinner.

Gather Ingredients

1 Zucchini
1 Carrot
1 T Olive oil

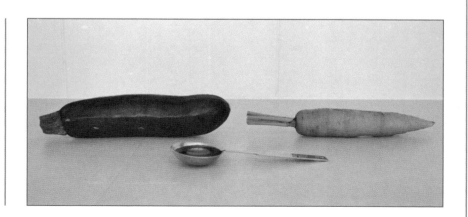

1 Wash zucchini and carrot.

2 Peel skin off carrot.

3 Continue to peel the entire carrot and add to bowl.

4 Peel zucchini down to the core and add to bowl.

5 Add oil.

6 Mix.

7 Place in pan on medium heat.

8 Stir until cooked, and serve.

Quesadillas

This simple and satisfying meal is a great introduction to cooking with heat.

Gather Ingredients

1 Tortilla
Cheddar cheese

| Grate cheese.

2 Place cheese on one half of the tortilla.

3 Fold the tortilla in half.

4 Place in pan and cook until brown.

5 Flip and cook the other side.

6 Remove from pan and serve.

Add other ingredients like mushrooms or bell peppers.

Try This!

Yummy Chocolate Cake

Indulge the occasional sweet tooth with Caspar's favorite recipe for chocolate cake.

Gather Ingredients

1 c Self-rising flour
3 T Cocoa
½ c Sugar
2 Eggs
¼ c Olive oil
¼ c Milk
Powdered sugar
   and sprinkles
   (optional)

1 Trace the bottom of the cake pan onto baking paper.

2 Cut out baking paper.

3 Line cake pan with baking paper.

4 Add flour to bowl.

5 Add cocoa to bowl.

6 Add sugar to bowl.

7 Crack eggs and add to bowl.

8 Add oil to bowl.

9 Add milk to bowl.

10 Mix all ingredients well.

11 Pour mixture into 8-inch cake pan.

12 Set timer to 30 minutes.

13 Have an adult bake in the oven at 350°F or 180°C for 30 minutes.

14 Cool cake on a cooling rack.

15 Dust with powered sugar and colored sprinkles.

16 Serve.

What Comes Next?

In this book, we've tried to provide a comprehensive, step-by-step guide for cultivating confidence, competence, and independence in the kitchen (while having fun!). To continue your child's development in the kitchen, consider helping them to:

Cut-up fruit with toothpicks makes an easy snack to share.

Expand Their Recipe Repertoire Perhaps you could help them create a binder or a recipe box with new recipes they would like to try.

Host a Party Your child can share his/her new culinary talents by hosting a small get-together and preparing all the treats.

Invent New Recipes Your child might have their own ideas about what flavors and ingredients work well together. Encourage this kind of innovation and experimentation. Be sure to record what works! Perhaps your child can put together his or her own cookbook?

Beyond the kitchen, there are many ways to involve your child in the practical life activities of the home that will help them develop confidence, competence, and a strong sense of self-worth. Think about what the adults in the family do to keep the household functioning and figure out ways to involve your children in those day-to-day tasks. Children from a very young age can be involved in tasks, such as:

When we involve children from a very early age in the practical considerations of our family life, they internalize deep self-worth.

Self-Care Children can start dressing themselves at a very early age if you provide the right amount of support. Consider setting out two different outfit choices and letting them select what they would like to wear. They can also comb their own hair and brush their own teeth.

Laundry Children can help collect dirty laundry, carry it to the washing machine in a child-sized basket, and put items into the washing machine or pull them from the dryer. They can also be involved with the folding. Of course their folds won't look as perfect as yours, but the process is more important than the product.

Cleaning With the right child-sized products, children can do nearly everything that adults do. They can dust, sweep, vacuum, clean windows, wipe down tables, mop, wash dishes, polish silver or wood, etc.

Setting the Table Children can easily help set the table if you provide a placemat that indicates where everything goes. You can embroider the separate spots, or you could use applique to mark out where the plate, fork, spoon, knife, and cup go.

Plant and Animal Care With support and guidance, children can learn to take care of the plants and animals in the home. They can feed dogs, cat, fish, etc. They can refill water bowls. They can water plants or clean off dusty leaves with a small sponge or cloth.

Whenever you want to involve your child in practical life, remember to teach your child the activity first, rather than just expect them to be able to do it. Consider these questions:

☐ How can I break this activity down into the simplest steps?

☐ How can I model all the steps in the slowest, clearest way possible?

☐ How can I reteach this lesson if my child needs additional support?

This approach to helping our children be contributing members of our families takes immense time, patience, and forethought, but the investment is worth it. When we involve children from a very early age in the practical considerations of our family life, they internalize deep self-worth. When we start early, we don't have to pay our children to do things that the adults are doing for free. It simply becomes part of the norm; it becomes what we all do to help out our family unit.

What is Montessori?

Maria Montessori was Italy's first female physician. After attending medical school in the early 1900s, she found her way into education. She applied her scientific and empirical nature to the first school she founded in the slums of Italy in 1907. She closely observed children and their needs and developed an educational framework serving children from birth to age 24. More than a century later, there are Montessori schools from birth through high school across the globe.

The Montessori approach to education helps children reach their fullest potential and find their place in the world, so that they can lead lives full of meaning and joy and create a more peaceful world.

Specifically, the Montessori approach helps cultivate the following:

☐ Focus and Concentration ☐ Global Awareness

☐ Independence and Self-Confidence ☐ Appreciation for the Environment

☐ Curiosity and Lifelong Learning ☐ Empathy and Kindness

☐ Perseverance ☐ A Peaceful World

The *Wall Street Journal* coined the phrase "Montessori Mafia" to describe the fact that many members of the "creative elite" attribute their success to their experience in Montessori schools. Famous Montessorians include the founders of Google, Amazon.com, and Wikipedia, as well as Julia Child and P. Diddy. Historical examples of famous Montessorians include Anne Frank and Jackie Kennedy Onassis.

Being a Montessori parent can seem more difficult initially because it requires immense time and patience to support children as they develop their independence. However, you will reap the rewards as your child develops increased independence.

Meet Caspar

Caspar is four years old and loves to cook and play outside.

Caspar cooked, taste-tasted and approved every recipe. His favorite is the Yummy Chocolate Cake.

Tasks like using the toilet and doing chores become everyday things rather than struggles that require extrinsic motivation like star charts and candy.

If you would like to learn more about Montessori, we encourage you to explore the resources listed in the Appendix, in addition to calling a local Montessori school and scheduling a visit. When you look for a school to observe, be aware that the word "Montessori" is not trademarked and can be used by anyone. The best way to ensure the authenticity of the Montessori school is to inquire about teacher certification. Teachers who are trained by the Association Montessori Internationale (AMI) or the American Montessori Society (AMS) have undergone rigorous training about Montessori philosophy and curriculum implementation.

Appendix

Resources for more information:

Books Hughes, Kathi, *Learning Together: What Montessori Can Offer Your Family*, The Montessori St Nicholas Charity; 1st edition (2012)

Montanaro, Silvana Quattrocchi, *Understanding the Human Being (Clio Montessori)*, A B C Clio; 5th Edition edition (1992)

Montessori, Maria, *The Absorbent Mind*, BN Publishing (2009)

Polk Lillard, Paula, *Montessori Today: A Comprehensive Approach to Education from Birth to Adulthood*, Schocken (1996)

Polk Lillard, Paula and Lynn Lillard Jessen, *Montessori from the Start: The Child at Home, from Birth to Age Three*, Schocken; 1 edition (2003)

Seldin, Tim and Vanessa Davies, *How To Raise An Amazing Child the Montessori Way*, DK Adult (2006)

Stoll Lillard, Angeline, *Montessori: The Science Behind the Genius*, Oxford University Press, USA; Updated edition (2008)

Booklets North American Montessori Teachers, *In a Montessori Home*, www.montessori-namta.org/Print-Publications/Parent-Education/In-a-Montessori-Home

North American Montessori Teachers, *At Home with Montessori (Ages 3-6)*, www.montessori-namta.org/Print-Publications/Parent-Education/At-Home-with-Montessori-ages-3-6

Websites
www.montessorihomes.blogspot.com
www.howwemontessori.com
www.feedingthesoil.com
www.montessorionthedouble.com/blog
www.mariamontessori.com
www.aidtolife.org

Videos *Edison's Day*, www.montessori-namta.org/DVDs-and-Videos/Edisons-Day

Montessori Madness, by Trevor Eissler www.youtube.com/watch?v=GcgN0lEh5IA

Vendors Beginning Montessori, beginningmontessori.com

For Small Hands, forsmallhands.com

Goose Designs, etsy.com/shop/goosedesigns

Handmade Montessori Materials, etsy.com/shop/montessori

Michael Olaf, michaelolaf.net

Montessori House, etsy.com/shop/MontessoriHouse

Montessori Services, montessoriservices.com

Australia and New Zealand
Montessori Child, montessorichild.com.au

Montessori Shop, montessorishop.co.nz

Made in the USA
Lexington, KY
02 January 2014